O'de
June

GAL JUNIE

ISBN: 9798397162043
ISBN-13:

Cover designed by Bookworms Anonymous LLC
https://www.facebook.com/BookwormsAnonymous1

Interior Illustrations by Gal Junie, Rachael Nash and Emma Henry
Music laid out by Jeff and Suzanne Henry
'Poor Old Joe' music laid out by Fernando Himenez

DEDICATION

For My Family

a little bit of glamour
a little bit of fun
a little joke, a little laugh
a little ray of sun
i hope you like this little book
for what I've tried to do
is show the things I like a lot –
a little bit like you
(1996)

CONTENTS

ACKNOWLEDGMENTS

I would like to acknowledge all the interesting people in my life, especially my own children and grandchildren.

You make for great poetry!

POEMS &
ODES

THE AUNTIE EDIE ODE

Aunt Edie had a hard life, she was widowed in her prime.
She had two sons to cater for and she worked hard all the time

She'd not sit feeling sorry for that was not her way.
She got a job in a café and she worked there night and day.

She cooked the dinners, washed the floor, made the tea and what is more,
She peeled the spuds and buttered bread and always smiled and never
said
That she was tired and needed rest for Edie always did her best.

Then one day they gave her the sack but two weeks later cried "come back"
For though two women worked all day – just half the hours for twice the pay –

Though they were two instead of one, they couldn't do what Edie' done.
So "come back Edie, come back do",

But Edie answered "[raspberry] to you"

But Edie was hard up poor gal so she got a job at the hospital
And there her duties grew and grew with jobs that others wouldn't do

And while the nobs came in their car (although they lived not very far)
Poor Edie pedalled on her bike through fog and ice and freezing night

One day arriving at the door with feet wet through and bottom sore,
She planned to make a cup of tea for "that will warm me up" thought she.

One woman (who was quite a snob) said "now you're going to lose your job"
And on poor Edie she did tell but Edie went along as well

And as poor Edie put her case her bosses knew they'd not replace her
The other woman had to go and Edie told her "[raspberry] to you"

Retiring from the hospital she'd been so economical
She hadn't spent much on herself and thus accumulated wealth

But then poor Edie passed away and her relations said "Hooray,
We'll go out and have a splash" but they could not find Edie's cash.

"Wherever can it be?" they said and to the cemetery they sped
In case her gravestone held a clue and there they read it "[raspberry] to you"

So if someone upsets you, you know what to do –
Be like Auntie Edie and tell them "[RASPBERRY] TO YOU!"

WHO TOLD YOU LOT TO LAUGH?

Who told you lot to laugh?
That's what I want to know
The weather's very windy
And tomorrow it might snow.

You know your boots are leaking
And your tights are laddered too
But still you keep on laughing
Whatever's the matter with you?

Who told you lot to laugh?
There's no tea in the pot
You think the water's boiling
But it isn't even hot.

Your biscuits aren't McVities
The one's you've got are soggy
And should you want a wee-wee
There's no loo roll in the boggy.

Who told you lot to laugh?
They don't leave you a sight.
What they give you with their left hand
They take back with their right.

The pensions gone up
But so has the rent
So when you receive it
It's already spent

But I must keep cheerful
If you lot insist
For I can't stop you laughing
You're all round the twist!

WAITRESSING DUTIES

With my waitressing duties to be done (to be done)
And serving tables really ain't much fun (ain't much fun)
I would rather be on page three in The Sun (in The Sun)
A waitress lot is not a happy one (happy one)

Have you seen the man at table two?
I don't believe he's with his wife, do you?
He called her 'Love', she called him 'Dear'
I don't believe he's having his afters here!

Oh did you know my dear, a streaker came in here
Sat down upon a chair, serve him I didn't dare.
Made quite an impression, lifted my depression,
I'd like another session; he's coming back next week.
"Next week, what a cheek! Can I have a peek?"

With the bread tucked underneath me arm I staggered through the door
Perspiration was dripping off me nose and me feet were sore
A man had ordered bread and soup, he looked to be a toff-
I said "you haven't got a hope – bread's off"
And being quite the gentleman he gave a discreet cough and said
"The bread's tucked underneath your arm."

There was I waiting at the till
No one paid their bill
They'd been taken ill
Someone telephoned for the old Bill
And they had me arrested (rested)
Judge refused to let me out on bail
Said my food was stale
Threw me in the jail
Can't get away to open my café but I'm not complaining.

BOB A JOB

A terrorist held the hostage
With a gun against his head
The hooded man from the SAS
Prepared to shoot him dead
  The woman in the bus queue said
  "You're gonna have a job"
  And the boy scout said
  "I'll do it for a bob"
The pensioner was broke again
The day his rent was due
"If I saw the Prime Minister
I'd tell 'em a thing or two"
  The woman in the bus queue said
  "You're gonna have a job"
  And the boy scout said
  "I'll do it for a bob"
Unmercifully the judge peered down
And gave the prisoner life
"I want to start a family"
Appealed his sobbing wife
  The woman in the bus queue said
  "You're gonna have a job"
  And the boy scout said
  "I'll do it for a bob"
The pensioner was broke AGAIN
His hopes were fading lower
"If I saw the Prime Minister
I'd lock 'em in the Tower"
  The woman in the bus queue said
  "You're gonna have a job"
  And the boy scout said
  "I'll do it for a bob".

LONESOME TONIGHT

I'm so lonesome tonight
And my bra is too tight
And my corsets are falling apart.

And I've got a big chest
It's made holes in my vest
And my spare tyre goes right past my heart.

And my stockings are laddered
My shoes worn and thin
And my knickers held up with a big safety pin.

Now my false teeth are worn
So they drop when I yawn
Tell me why I'm so lonesome tonight?

I'LL SING A SONG

I'll sing a song called Tipperary
I'll sing a song called Moonlight Bay
We'll have the boys sing Yankee Doodle
And then I'll give you Dolly Grey
And then we'll catch up with some drinking
So we can sing till break of day
Yes we'll sing all night long and then…
Just one more song and I'll be on my way.

DOMINIC

There was a boy named Dominic
He sucked a lolly to the stick
He ate a burger, peas and fries
And half a dozen apple pies.
He licked around the honey jar
And polished off a chocolate bar.
He bought an icecream, took a lick
And then the boy called Dominic
Was SICK!

LITTLE OLD LADY

Little old lady passing by
Catching everyone's eye
She has such a charming manner, sweet and shy

Little old lady cautiously, takes a snip from a tree
Has a pair of secateurs that no one else can see
Little snip of something here
Little tug at something there
No one seems to notice as their plants all disappear

Little old lady at the show
Where the top growers go
Snip, snip, snip their plants are gone
But where they do not know

Little old lady out to dine
Has a smile so divine
Thinks, "Those flowers in that vase will soon be mine"

Flowers are gone now fancy that
Someone thinks it is the cat
Little old lady sits there with them all tucked in her hat
Waiter says what's going on
Where have all my flowers gone?
Little old lady says, "I must be going, can't stay out too long"

Little old lady in the city
Where the flowers are so pretty
Tug, tug, tug they're in her bag while she says "What a pity"

Once Prince Charlie passed her by
Followed by Lady Di
Little old lady stood there looking oh so shy
Little old lady she was mean
Curtsied low to the Queen
Nicked the rose right off her hat and wasn't even seen
Princess Anne said, "What a lorse, must have been my stupid horse

Knew he must be getting puckish as I rode him round the course."
Little old lady's garden gay
It's the best one they say
Little old lady's fast asleep – she's had a busy day.

21

MY OLD MAN'S SNOOKER TABLE

On my old man's snooker table there's a dinner laid for four
There's a bucket full of soapy suds I used to wash the floor.

There's a pile of washing from the line, a dishcloth from the sink
A piece of strong elastic and a pair of knickers—pink.

There's a fiver for the milkman and a saucer with some lard on
A bone saved for the dog next door and some compost for the garden.

Some linctus if you have a cough, a coupon with some money off
A pile of string to be untwisted, a bill with all the shopping listed.

A pile of dirty saucepan lids, a dozen fruit buns for the kids
Some underpants all nice and clean, a letter written to the Queen.

A bunion plaster for the feet, a remedy for prickly heat,
A water bottle for the bed, a jar of asprin for the head.

Some sausage rolls the old man likes, wheel off someone's motor bike.

Now in the snooker pockets there are apples for a tart
A pound of Spanish onions and some beans that make you break wind.

There's a ball of wool, a glove, a hat, a sock a shoe, a lump of fat.

A piece of cheese, some Vaseline, some paste to keep the false teeth
clean.

A pot of Vick to ease congestion
A tablet that will help digestion.

A bottle that is full of gin to make you feel elated
A dish that has some rhubarb in, in case you're constipated.

And on the end that I have seen as fit to keep my sewing machine
A pile of things of granny's which are waiting to receive a stitch.

There's jumble for the poor and needy, a lettuce that has gone all seedy.

And in the room where they play pool, I've stored a dozen sacks of coal
Some kindling wood inside a sack, a box that's full of nutty slack.

The kids have left a football there, some wet and smelly swimming gear
The dog is in his beanbag bed – he's either fast asleep or dead.

My old man doesn't say much, but you know what he's like
He just stuck his cue right up my nose and rode off on his bike!

AT BEJAMS STORE

At Bejams store for days or more
Quite orderly in through the door
The people came, the people went
Their purchase made, their money spent

Then suddenly who should burst in
Both middle-aged, one fat one thin
The Mrs Henrys, one and two
One never knew what they would do

And crying out, "Oh no, not them!"
The manager rushed to his den
He turned the key inside the door
And stayed there for an hour or more

The cleaning lady was in tears
She'd faithfully cleaned up for years
She said, "One day I'll flip instead
And shove this pail on someone's head"

A pretty wench sat at the till
And soon her eyes with tears did fill
Her true love turned out a swine
And never sent a Valentine

Around the store as if on wings
Complaining of the price on things
The sisters shoved their trolleys round
And sent display stands to the ground

The manager sat on his a---
Safely entombed behind plate glass
Surveyed the havoc in the room
Sent his assistant out with broom

Some pensioners who'd been outside
Jumped in the trolleys for a ride
Then all went rushing round the store
And had a picnic by the door

The manager said with a cry
"You can't come in unless you buy"
To pensioners I never shout
So spend your money or "GET OUT"

They asked the price of one fish finger
For his reply they did not linger
And as the words formed on his lips
They blew their pension on some chips

As finally they left the store
The Henrys, two and one
Both felt though they were penniless
It had been lots of fun

Although this is a load of squit
We hope you'll like it just a bit
And if you do, well sad to say
You'll end up just like us one day!

ODE TO SMOKEY JOE

I wonder if some legal bloke
Might clarify the law on smoke
I tell you boy that in't no joke
To live near Smokey Joe

We moan about the sewerage smell
At least we know it's na-tur-el
But what's he burning? Who can tell?
What is it Smokey Joe?

I find it somewhat consternating
A bonfire war is escalating
Is everyone retaliating
Against old Smokey Joe?

I asked my friend "Is something wrong?
You come round but you don't stay long"
She said, "I just can't stand the pong
That comes from Smokey Joe's"

Some mornings when the weather's fine
I hang my drawers out on the line
And then he lights a fire – the swine –
I curse that Smokey Joe

It may be that some native bloke
Could read a message in the smoke
A social worker might evoke
Some help for Smokey Joe

The neighbours then with some elation
Might contribute a good donation
To send him to a reservation
Goodbye to Smokey Joe

Then from his work he could retire
To sit all day beside the fire
Till, nicely tanned, he would expire
What joy for Smokey Joe

And everyone would ask round here
"Whatever is this stuff, my dear?"
And I would answer "Thas fresh air –
Untouched by Smokey Joe"

SIX TO SIXTY

When you are six and your legs say "GO"
And Mum and Dad say "NO, NO, NO"
And Teacher says "NO WAY, NO WAY"
Then will you still run out and play?

And when you are the big SIX-O
And your dreams say "OK – LET'S GO"
Those same old legs creak out, "NO WAY"
Then should you GO or should you STAY?

So here I sit and wonder why
Must we be good until we die?
And if we don't will you and I
Join Rabbit in McGregor's pie
Or be like Peter Pan and FLY?

And poor old me, I'm getting weak
If I jump up my joints all creak
And when I say "OK – Let's GO"
My creaky legs say, "NO, NO, NO"

BOY CHARLIE (THE PLASTERER)

Boy Charlie was a plasterer – worked on a building site
He went boozing every dinner time and drinking every night

Then one day after Charlie'd supped twenty pints of beer
He got chucked out of the Bridge House pub but Charlie didn't care

A pub called the Red Lion was just across the street
And a little smile lit up his face as he struggled to his feet

Then twenty cars went whizzing by and twenty buses too
Poor Charlie couldn't cross the road and wondered what to do

And then, just for a minute, a taxi cab stopped there
And when the taxi'd pulled away boy Charlie'd disappeared

Not having had a fare all day the driver thought "That's good"
Asked Charlie "Where to Guvnor?" Charlie said "Across the road"

And then Boy Charlie fell asleep which really was a pity
And the meter ticked away the pounds as they drove around the city

First the inner ring road they went six times round
Then off to Harford Bridges and back to the football ground

And then they stopped at Carrow Road with Delia Smith outside
With her first team of eleven men who all sat there and cried

For though they'd tried their very best they hadn't scored one goal
Against the team they'd played that day from the local infants' school

Then off they drove to the City Hall and there beside the market
The taxi driver left the car as he'd found a place to park it

Beside St Mancroft they'd pulled up with a lurch
And Charlie woke in time to see a bride rush from the church

"I'm in a hurry" she cried out "my baby's overdue,
And as the groom has got cold feet I'll have to marry YOU"

So when Boy Charlie sobered up he knew not what to do
Not only was he married – he'd become a Daddy too.

And knowing he could booze no more, to the building site he went
And sadly threw himself into a mixer of cement

And now he's set in concrete just like a garden gnome
If you pass by you'll see him there outside a stately home

Now little dogs look up at him and for a bone they beg
And then when they don't get one they do things up his leg

So let this be a warning to all of you who drink
You may end up plastered in more ways that you think!

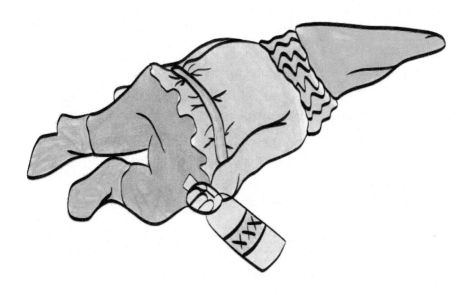

BUNGAY BEANS AND BRAN

It's windy down in Bungay town
It's windy as can be
And everything is blowing off
But none more so than me.

Oh I went down to Bungay town
A diet for to get
The doctor took one look at me
And put me on 'Plan F'

I started eating beans and bran
And sad to tell you dearie
Though I was fit, I ponged a bit
My friends would not come near me

Now Connie was a Bonnie lass
Till she went on a diet
The doctor put her on 'Plan F'
If just to keep her quiet

So Connie ate her beans and bran
Until the other night
She blasted into orbit
And now she's a satellite

Once Margaret Thatcher came to see
The doc to learn her fate
She thought that she was pregnant
She was only overweight

The doctor put her on 'Plan F'
Which really was a pity
For now I hear she's only just
A BIG NOISE in the City

A Coleman's lass to Bungay went
On her promotion drives
And now the doctor's scrapped 'Plan F'
And gives you mustard pies

So if to Bungay you should go
And get his mustard pies
If I were you I'd let him have one
Right between the eyes.

(1983)

THE BEST JAM

They had a little problem at the T.W.G.
To judge the competition well I'm glad no one asked me!
The contest was for homemade jam, they had to get it right
There must be no hint of cheating or we'd end up with a fight.
There were plenty who were willing to say how it should be done—
Telling how to pick the winning jam and say why it had won.
You had to hold it upside down then you could surely bet,
If it ran out all over you it wasn't properly set.
You had to taste a spoonful and a dozen ladies did,
Till just one little bit was left stuck on the jam jar lid.
Next they all got in a huddle and decided with some passion
That jam was better in the war when things were on the ration.
One lady said it wasn't bad, another one was heard
To say it was disgusting and that she liked lemon curd.
The chairlady then shouted out "my kids will want their dinner—
So I'll get these lot sorted out and say who is the winner!"
She cogitated, ruminated, scratched her head and hesitated,
Paused and then deliberated, read her stars and then she stated…
"There's only been one entry, Mrs Harrison's I heard,
So I suggest we make her FIRST, SECOND AND THIRD!
Thank you"

PAINTING THINGS

Gal Joycie's fond a painting things
She doesn't mind what they are
She'll paint anything from thimble
To a Rolls Royce motor car

She goes to all the jumble sales
And buys the pots and pans
And she goes clanging down the street
With all her rusty cans

There's jugs upon the mantlepiece—
That's where she dries them out
There's buckets on the piano
And it makes her old man shout

Once he opened up the oven
And said, "Ah, a casserole"
Said Joyce, "Don't you switch that on
That's my newly painted bowl."

So she puts things in the pantry
When she don't know where to hide 'em
And her old man throws the cans about
When he finds no food inside 'em.

Now Winnie up at number two
Has an old tin chamber pot
And she likes to keep it 'neath her bed
Cos she do feel queer a lot.

But when Joycie done her cleaning
She had to hurry to the loo
For she couldn't use the chamber pot–
It was painted pink and blue.

Now Reggie came home from the pub
And he lives at eighty-eight
And he only knew which house was his
Cause it had a purple gate.

But on the day in question
Joyce went round with paint in tin
And Reggie's gate was now bright green
So he didn't dare go in.

In the morning when his missus cried
"You've come home ten hours late"
He said, "Well blame gal Joycie—
She's painted ruddy gate."

MR WILLIAMS

I got a job at Laurence Scott
I liked it a little but not a lot
None of the men were particularly hot
But I got MR WILLIAMS

He lost his glasses twice a day
He lost his pen I'd hear him say
"Oh damn, oh bugger, oh gawd, oh blast"
(I had a feeling I wouldn't last)

"Make me a coffee," I'd hear him say
Two or three times every day
"Make it sweet," I'd hear him mutter
"Strong and black and fill the cuppa"
"Sweet and black and every day
Just how I like my women," he'd say

Sweet and black and strong and hot
Yes that's the man I wish I'd got
The time I worked for Laurence Scott
But I got MR WILLIAMS!
(1979)

TURN THE SILVER, LILLY

Many, many years ago
Lilly was a sickly child
The doctors said, "There's little hope"
And Lilly's mother cried
"Now see this silver sixpence
I give to you today?
Keep it with you always, Lilly
And remember what I say"
        Turn the silver, Lilly
        There's a sliver moon tonight
        Turn the silver, Lilly
        Things will surely turn out right
        You mustn't view it first through glass
        So go beyond the door
        And turn the silver, Lilly
        And the pain will be no more.
Now through the many troubles
Lilly found within her life
She did the very best she could
As mother and as wife
To every crying infant
She held upon her knee
She said, "Listen and I'll tell you
What my mother told to me"
        Turn the silver, Lilly
        There's a sliver moon tonight
        Turn the silver, Lilly
        Things will surely turn out right
        You mustn't view it first through glass
        So go beyond the door
        And turn the silver, Lilly
        And the pain will be no more.

I made a call on Lilly
Only just the other day
And in her weary gnarled old hand
Her silver sixpence lay
And through the open window
The new moon shone far away
And I turned the sixpence over
Just as Lilly passed away
   Turn the silver, Lilly
   There's a sliver moon tonight
   Turn the silver, Lilly
   Things will surely turn out right
   You mustn't view it first through glass
   So go beyond the door
   And turn the silver, Lilly
   And the pain will be no more.

(1984)

TENNIS

I've been in trouble lately and I couldn't pay my dues.
My problems really started when I bought a pair of shoes.

Then I squandered all my housekeeping on things like milk and bread
And stayed up to watch the tele when I should have gone to bed

But I think what really done me was the final luxury
I threw all caution to the wind and bought some jam for tea

They put me up before the judge he was quite a simpleton
He said, "She must be sent to court." So I went to Wimbledon

I took my do-do tablets to make certain I was fit
But they weren't quite working properly so I got the runs a bit

So just as a precaution (I knew what I was about)
I put elastic in my drawers so nothing could fall out

Yes I went to play at Wimbledon against Navratilova
I bent to pull my knickers up and a ball came flying over

The umpire shouted, "15-love" I said, "Well thank you, dear
But actually I'm 48 – it's the way I do my hair"

Navratilova called the boy another ball to get
I said, "Don't send that over here, I int found the first one yet"

She gave me such a funny look but paid me no attention
Then served the ball and hit me in a place too rude to mention

I said, "Look here you mawther, this time you've gone too far"
The umpire said, "Where is that ball?" I said, "Here in me bra"

The umpire shouted, "Thirty love." I said, "No, I'm forty-eight"
And then she served another ball and I cried, "Why can't you wait?"

The umpire shouted, "Forty love." I was ageing very fast
I said, "Look here, I'm forty-eight." And a ball came whizzing past.

Then McEnroe came charging up shouting, "Have you seen my ball?"
I said, "Look in your trousers." But there weren't one there at all.

He said, "This isn't funny, you really are the pits."
And I said, "Why don't you clear off? You're getting on my—nerves."

I was chatting up the umpire when a shot came from a gun
And McEnroe had killed him dead so I don't know if I won.

And then they said that every year they'd pay a thousand quid
If I would sign a contract so that is what I did.

They pay an awful lot of cash for stars to come and play
But I'm the only tennis star who's paid to stay away.
1984

YOUNG OR OLD

It's nice when you are young and strong to hurry to and fro
To do a thousand thrilling things and laugh where 'ere you go.
It's nice when you are growing old and there seems nothing new
To sit and think of all the things which once you used to do.

THE JUMBLE SALE ODE

Every Saturday afternoon if you'd like to think of me
At a jumble sale with Joyce and Flo and Irish Mary I'll be

With our pockets full of change and a shopping bag or two
Our insurance policies paid up and a comfortable flat shoe

Skinheads at a football match may think they're rather tough
But five minutes down our rummage sale they find they've had enough

Now being short I sometimes wait for a minute at the back
But once I thought "That's got dark early, everything's gone black"

But some great flippin' mawther had given me a wack
And shoved me with her jumble inside a dustbin sack

I tell you for a minute the air in there was blue
I said, "Go and join the SAS they want recruits like you"

A pair of bloomers were 5p and Mary knocked them up to 10
So she got an Irish bargain and they all said, "Come again"

Then Mary saw a saucepan and asked me, "How much should I pay?"
And Joyce said, "Make an offer love that work out best that way"

Mary said, "How much with you offer?" and the seller said "A quid"
And Mary said, "Done" and I said, "You are cos that int got a lid"

Then Joycie bought a teapot and I said, "Now that's a rummin—
There's a great big hole in the bottom gal, they musta seen you cummin"

I bought myself a chamber pot but that won't go'neath the bed
I keep it on the window sill with a plant in it instead

And Flo, she got a bathing suit, on the beach she's a sensation
She said, "That's full a moth holes but I like the ventilation

So when you give for the rummage sale, a gift however humble
Joyce or Mary, Flo or June we'll buy it down the JUMBLE.
1982

FISHERMAN OF WALCOTT

He often can be seen afloat
Fishing in his wee blue boat
He may catch cod or bass or ling—
Some days he won't catch anything
He may catch mackerel or dabs
He might inspect his pots for crabs
We hear him boil them in his copper
And shout, "Mary, I've a whopper"
And Mary cried, "For goodness sake—
I've got a really bad headache
I've put some tinnies by your chair
Just sit and watch your gee-gees dear
I see you've filleted the dabs
So I'll just sit and scrub your crabs"
With all the joys that God invented
Here sits a man who's most contented
No happier man could there ever be
Than the fisherman of Walcott-on-sea!
(1996)

FOR PERCY IN THE BICYCLE SHOP

When it's raining hard and you've got a cough
And your brakes are worn and your chain fell off
Don't stand and say "oh-ah, oh-ah"
Have a little sweetie from the jar.

When there's lots of bills lying on the mat
And your bell won't ring and your tyres are flat
Don't stand and say "oh-ah, oh-ah"
Have a little sweetie from the jar.

When your belt is worn and your braces snap
And your pants fall down and you've lost your cap
Don't stand and say "oh-ah, oh-ah"
Have a little sweetie from the jar.

When the tax man comes and he makes a fuss
And no one loves you – only us
Don't stand and say "oh-ah, oh-ah"
Have a little sweetie from the jar.

A FISHY TALE – FROM WALCOTT-ON-SEA

(1999)
The wind was blowing, the tide was in
The sea was making such a din
But Micky Boy just sat there wishing
That it was nice enough for fishing.
He wrapped up warm to face the deep
And pulled his wellies on his feet.
Then what do you think that daft fool did?
He bought some lugworms – spent ten quid
He leaned right over the old sea wall
A wave came over and made him fall
He grumbled and mumbled, you can bet
His wellies were full, his trousers wet
He squeaked and squelched back down the lane
Until he got back home again
It was enough to make you weep –
Just like a monster from the deep
He gave the neighbours all a fright
So now they won't go out at night
The moral of the story's this…
Go down the chippie to get your fish.

LEGEND OF ROBBENS' BAY

This is the legend of Robbens' Bay
Where a fisherman lost his way
Only Sir Derek could cast his rod
He's put a curse on others – the sod!

Now on one very misty night
Mick was in for quite a fright
With lamp in hand to light his way
He sneaked off down to Robbens' Bay

He settled down to do some fishing
And then he saw an apparition
"Begone" it cried through lips of froth
"Pick up your rods and bugger off!"

With knocking knees Mick grabbed his gear
A ghostly chuckle he did hear
A smell of Guinness in the air
And on the wall and empty glass of beer

We hope the moral won't be missed –
If you believe this – YOU ARE PISSED!

MINI POEMS

Please buy my lucky heather
This heather is alright
Grown at Walcott-by-the-sea
At my new camping site

My pegs will hang onto your wash
No matter how the winds do blow
So make yourself a lucky man
And cross my palm with silver NOW

I am a little hag-stone
And good luck will be yours.
Thread me with a ribbon
And hang me by your door.
The sea has taken centuries
To wear this hole away.
Now I keep away all evil
Or so the Nor-folk say.
(As featured in Redway Acres)

When the days are bright it's a lovely sight
To go down to the sea so blue
But it gives you a fright on a windy night
When the sea tries to visit you!

RONNIE'S FISHING HAT

I'll never forget that old fishing hat.
It belonged to my brother called Ron.
It laid in the shed, like a cat that was dead,
And it had a peculiar pong.

I thought it was grey till that fateful washday
—a day oh so sunny and fine.
I'd boiled all my whites and my knickers and tights
Were billowing out on the line.

And I'd washed all the frocks and the pants and the socks,
But I still had some nice soapy water.
And I looked at the hat (it annoyed me did that)
But I thought, "No perhaps I don't oughta."

Then I soaked my poor feet, oh that was a treat,
For the soapsuds were lovely and hot.
Next the curtains went in, then the old pedal bin.
Then I scrubbed out my old chamber pot.

But each time I went out to the line I was drawn,
To the hat in the shed lying there all forlorn.
Lying there caked with mud, thick with grease and obscene.
And I itched when I saw it to get that hat clean.

'Twas a day that I had to get everything clean.
So, I threw that old hat in the washing machine.
And as it was washed biologically,
The dirt that came out was a pleasure to see.

And that hat wasn't grey. It was green, red and blue.
It was checked with all colours—a beautiful hue!
And it dried on the line as the sun shone and shone
I was proud of that hat when I showed it to Ron.
"What the hell have you done to my hat?
Took me ages to get it like that!

I've dropped it in cow pats, worn it in rain,
Dragged it through bushes, again and again.
I blended in nice with the river did that—
Fish'll see me for miles in this bloody clean hat!"

Then he threw that hat high, threw it high in the air,
And he stormed down the pub for a skinful of beer.

Behind the coal bunker it went, and there it did stay.
And I happen to know that it's still there today.
It's rotten and smelly, disgusting to see.
Full of cobwebs and spiders and pussy cats' pee.

But I'm wrapping it nicely when Ron's birthday's here.
"I've got a nice present," I'll say, "for you dear."
"It's something you'll treasure, I'm certain of that.
I know that you'll love it. IT'S A NICE FISHING HAT!"
(1980)

SONGS

(I Don't Believe in) Happy Ever After

Gal Junie

I don't be-lieve in ha-ppy e-ver af-ter. I won't be here for

e-ver af-ter a-ny-how. I don't be-lieve in ha-ppy e-ver af-ter.

Love me now. 1. They told the sol-dier when the war was o-ver
2. You say you will re-turn some day to love me

He'd see the blue-birds o'er the cliffs of Do-ver They frigh-tened off the
Boy, on that day the grass will grow a-bove me The flow-ers may be

blue-birds as they drilled the sea for oil But li-ttle cared the sol-dier bu-ried
bloo-ming well but, I'll be bloo-ming gone And you will find a-no-ther love to

'neath the fo-reign soil. I don't be-lieve in ha-ppy e-ver af-ter. I
show-er kiss-es on.

won't be here for e-ver af-ter a-ny-how. I don't be-lieve in ha-ppy e-ver

af-ter. Love me now.

HAPPY EVER AFTER

I don't believe in happy ever after
I won't be here for ever after anyhow
I don't believe in happy ever after
Love me now.

They told the soldier when the war was over
He'd see the bluebirds o'er the cliffs of Dover
They frightened off the bluebirds as they drilled the seas for oil
But little cared the soldier buried 'neath the foreign soil.

You say you will return some day to love me
Boy on that day the grass may grow above me
The flowers may be blooming well but I'll be blooming gone
And you will find another love to shower kisses on.

Old Palace Road

Gal Junie

I'm go-nna march up Old Pa-lace Road, I'm go-nna get the old place swing-ing And then I'll march down Old Pa-lace Road, And set the bells a ring dong ding-ing And then I'll march up Old Pa-lace Road, Till I hear all the peo-ple sing-ing You won't e-ven hear the neigh-bours com-plain Cos they'll be right behind me shout-ing 'Sing it a-gain' I feel so grand I feel I'll ex-plode. As I go march-ing; as I go march-ing; as I go march-ing down Old Pa-lace Road.

OLD PALACE ROAD

I'm gonna march up Old Palace Road
I'm gonna get the old place swinging
I'm gonna march up Old Palace Road
Till I hear all the people singing
And then I'll march down Old Palace Road
And set the bells a ring-dong-dinging
You won't even hear the neighbours complain
Cos they'll be right behind me shouting "sing it again"
I feel so grand I feel I'll explode
As I go marching, as I go marching as I go marching
Up Old Palace Road

The Old Bird Man of St Benedict's

Gal Junie

Have you seen the old bird-man of St Be-ne-dict's? He whist-les a - way all

day? Have you heard the old bird-man of St Be-ne-dict's;

whist-ling the blues a - way? Some times I'm sad, some times I'm

blue but I have to laugh when he comes in - to view For he'll whist-le for

me and he'll whist-le for you. That old bird - man of St Be-ne-dict's.

THE OLD BIRD MAN OF ST BENEDICTS

Have you seen the old bird man of St Benedicts?
He whistles away all day
Have you heard the old bird man of St Benedicts?
Whistling the blues away
Sometimes I'm sad, sometimes I'm blue
But I have to laugh when he comes into view
For he whistles for me and he'll whistle for you
The old bird man of St Benedicts.

Patricia's Kisses

June Henry

Pa - tri - cia kissed me once; Pa - tri - cia kissed me twice. I

find Pa - tri - cia's kiss - es oh so nice. Pa - tri - cia's kiss - es;

that's what I miss - es. I'm go - nna

get that gal to be my miss - us cos I just can't live with - out Pa-

- tri - cia's kiss - es. Tri - cia's kiss - es; that's what I

miss - es. I'm go - nna get that gal to

be my miss - us cos I just can't live with - out Pa - tri - cia's kiss - es. Tri - cia's

kiss - es.

PATRICIA'S KISSES

Patricia kissed me once
Patricia kissed me twice
I found Patricia's kisses oh so nice
Patricia's kisses, that's what bliss is
I gotta get that gal to be my missus
For I just can't live without Patricia's kisses, Tricia's kisses.

I asked her to come out
Knew what I was about
I knew that I just couldn't live without
Patricia's kisses, that's what bliss is
I gotta get that gal to be my missus
For I just can't live without Patricia's kisses, Tricia's kisses.

She says that she'll be mine
And now I'm feeling fine
Ain't been drinking whisky, ain't been drinking wine just
Tricia's kisses, that's what bliss is
I gotta get that gal to be my missus
For I just can't live without Patricia's kisses, Tricia's kisses.

Let's Go to War

June Henry

♩=160 Let's go to war, a-gainst the blues. This is the one war we can not a-fford to lose. We'll see a frown we'll chase it down; if we sing loud e-nough, we'll drive it out of town. Let's go to war, armed with a song. It's the best am-mu-ni-tion we can take a - long. You know we've got a - lot to be thank-ful for so let's all go to war!

LET'S GO TO WAR (AGAINST THE BLUES)

Let's go to war against the blues
This is the one that we cannot afford to lose
We'll see a frown, we'll chase it down
If we sing loud enough, we'll drive it out of town

Let's go to war, armed with a song
It's the best ammunition we can take along
You know we've got a lot to be thankful for
So let's all go to war.

Prices are high, troubles abound
No wonder why, blues are in town
Seems we can't win, still we must try
Not to give in, let's hear the cry

Let's go to war against the blues
This is the one that we cannot afford to lose
We'll see a frown, we'll chase it down
If we sing loud enough, we'll drive it out of town

Let's go to war, armed with a song
It's the best ammunition we can take along
You know we've got a lot to be thankful for
So let's all go to war.

Poor Old Joe

Gal Junie

OLD JOE
(as featured in Redway Acres)

I'm sitting quietly in my chair
They think I only sit and stare
But I don't miss much a sitting here
And here comes poor old Joe

Puts his money on the bar
Likes to buy us all a jar
Always asks yer, how y'are
But they don't ask poor old Joe

Seem to think he's a disgrace
Say he lowers the tone of the place
Wasn't born with a silver spoon in his face
So they don't want poor old Joe

He sits him down to drink his beer
They'd like to have him out of here
Don't like the way he wears his hair
No they don't like poor old Joe

They've got their problems too y'know
Say their profit margin's low
While they're keen to have his dough
They don't want poor old Joe

He's on his feet he's on his way
And as he leaves us every day
The only words you'll hear him say
Gawd bless yer, Gawd bless yer
But they don't like poor old Joe

I'm sitting quietly in my chair
They think I only sit and stare
Well, I don't miss much a sitting here
But I do miss poor old Joe

Gawd bless yer, Gawd bless yer
Gawd bless yer, POOR OLD JOE

Dodger's Cycle Shop

Gal Junie

1. At Dodger's cycle shop, that's where we like to stop. You can mend a
2. At Dodger's cycle place, there's nothing gone to waste. Ev-'ry things ace
3. At Dodger's cycle store, there's bits u - pon the floor. I would-n't know just

punc-tured tyre and there's a cy-cle you can hire. A-ny-thing that you re-quire; down at Do-dger's
ounted for; there's bits from nine-teen - fif - ty - four. Pi-ling up right to the door, down at Dodger's
where to start to try to find a cer-tain part. He's got it to a pro-per art, down at Dodger's

shop. He will on - ly charge a li-ttle fee; his gen - e - ros - i - ty is
place. If your bike is rus - ty from the rain, he'll lu - bri-cate the chain and
store. He'' make sure your rims have got a shine; your wheels are both in line; your

un - der gua-ran - tee. He'll make sure your screws are nice and tight; your han-dle bars are
make it go a - gain. If you find your lights have ceased to go Give him half a
steer-ing's feel-ing fine. He will keep your pe - dals free from rust and help you to ad-

(3)

right; your seat the pro-per height. 4. At Dodg-er's cy - cle shop; that's where we like to
mo'; he'll ad - just the dy - na - mo.
just your ca - bles if they bust

stop. Win - ter days and su - mmer nights; un - der - neath the ti - lley lights.

Pu-tting all the World to rights in Dodg-er's cy - cle shop.

AT DODGER'S CYCLE SHOP

At Dodger's cycle shop
That's where we like to stop
He will mend a punctured tyre
And there's a cycle you can hire
Anything that you require
Down at Dodger's shop

He will only charge a little fee
His generosity
Is under guarantee
He'll make sure your screws are nice and tight
Your handlebars are right
Your seat the proper height

At Dodger's cycle place
There's nothing goes to waste
Everything's accounted for
There's bits from 1954
Piling up right to the door
Down at Dodger's place

If your bike is rusty from the rain
He'll lubricate the chain
And make it go again
If you find your lights have ceased to go
Give him half a mo'
He'll adjust the dynamo

At Dodger's cycle store
There's bits upon the floor
I wouldn't know just where to start
To try to find a certain part
He's got it to a proper art
Down at Dodger's store.

He'll make sure your rims have got a shine
Your wheels are all in line
Your steering's feeling fine
He will keep your pedals free from rust
And help you to adjust
Your cables if they bust.

At Dodger's cycle shop
That's where I like to pop
Winter days and summer nights
Underneath the Tilley lights
Putting all the world to rights
In Dodger's cycle shop

VALENTINE,
BIRTHDAY
AND
CHRISTMAS

VALENTINES
(FROM GAL JUNIE TO HER GRANDCHILDREN)

2023

I don't know what to write to you
I've tried for years and years
Your family don't like me
They've driven me to tears.
Your Dad says I'm a dummy
As also does your Mummy
Your sister and her boyfriend Jack
Tied me up inside a sack
Then left me when the binmen came
My Granny said it was a shame
The binman said that he was sorry
But had to put me in his lorry
Gran cried "you are a nasty fella"
And bashed him with her um ber rella
She took me home to make me better
That's why I'm writing you this letter
With only one more year to go
DO YOU LOVE ME-YES OR NO?

Dear LILLY you're so lovely
I see you at the school
I saw you sledging at the park
You really did look C-O-O-L
I cycled round to your house I knocked upon the door
Your drumming made a LOT OF NOISE I fell upon the floor
I struggled up the driveway The snow was falling faster
When I got home to Mummy She went to get a plaster
She put a plaster on my nose
Another on my head
I'm feeling sorry for myself I'm going straight to bed
I think I'll kiss my teddy bear
BUT JUST YOU WAIT UNTIL NEXY YEAR!
Please be my VALENTINE

At last the time has come my lover
The end of our romance
I longed to be your Valentine
But didn't stand a chance
I've done my education
I've been to uni too
And feel I can no longer waste
So much time chasing you.
I even passed my driving test
And bought a little car
I'm going round the world next week
I hope it isn't far!
I'm sure to meet a lot of girls
So loving and so sweet
I hope they won't complain a lot
About my smelly feet!
And as the years go passing by
I know that I will miss you
I have but only one regret
I NEVER GOT TO KISS YOU!

Be my VALENTINE - PLEASE
When I got up this morning
I rushed down to the shed
I slipped upon some dog poo
And fell down on my head.
I found my bike was rusty
The wheels had fallen off
I long to see you Poppy
But then I got a cough.
I rushed round to the chemist shouting
"CAN YOU HELP ME PLEASE?"
I tripped up on his doorstep
That's how I grazed my knees.
He bandaged up my knees and then
He bandaged up my head.
He dosed me up with linctus
And he sent me home to bed.
I tried to see you Poppy
As you can plainly see
I love you so much Sweetheart
But our love is not to be!
Guess who?

I really love you EMMA
And I mean this most sincerely
That's why I send a Valentine
I always write one yearly.
There's lots of boys outside your house
I told them I would fight
I told them you were my girl
But they gave me such a fright
Then one of them tweaked my poor nose
And one sat on my tummy
And then I cried and they just laughed
So I ran home to Mummy.
When I come to call next year
With my Nana at my side
She will make those nasty boys
All run away and hide.
I'll have another problem then
And Emma this is it -
She won't let me go out with girls
She's teaching me to KNIT!!

I've saved my pocket money
To get you something sweet
But I don't know what I should buy
What do you like to eat?
Do you like eggs and bacon?
Do you like fish and chips?
Do you like chicken nuggets?
You must have greasy lips!
So if I try to kiss you
Will I slip off your chin?
And if I kiss your nose instead
A b-0-g-e-y might be in!
There's so much to consider
And it's harder than I thought
I'll just come round for dinner
And then share out what I've bought!
Your VALENTINE XXX

Dear EMILY you are so sweet
From the top of your head
To the toes on your feet.
You work so hard in all you do
That's why I fell in love with you.
And so I send you lots of Kisses
Flying far across the sea
I hope that you will love me too
And send your Kisses back to ME
From VALENTINE - guess who?

The tide comes in, the tide goes out
I sit here in my boat
I gaze through my binoculars
But see no one afloat.
I cast my bait into the sea
I wait then take a look
I catch some cod, some bass some plaice
But it's YOU I long to hook.
The North Sea can be very cold
But if you love me true
Why don't you swim around the coast?
I'm looking out for you.
I've got a fire going
There is smoked fish and a tinny
The MAN FROM THE EAST is waiting
To hold you dearest Lynnie.
I've loved you for so long my dear
Of that there is no doubt
I sit and wait so patiently
As the tide goes in and out

Dear Jack
2005
I'm feeling rather ill
I think I'll take a pill
My temperature is high
My throat is very dry
My heart is beating faster
I need a sticky plaster
I'm so in love with YOU
(unless I've caught the 'flu)
With love from your VALENTINE
XXX ??? XXX

Dear Molly -
You will get lots of Valentines
Because you are so sweet
You get more lovely every year
I hope that we can meet
I'd take you for a cycle ride
But someone nicked my bike
Or you could watch my football match
If that is what you'd like.
And after I could come round yours
And sit and watch T.V.
While you could scrub my muddy boots
And wash my kit for me.
With all these most romantic things
It will be hard to chose
So you stay in and wash your hair
While I go on the booze!
Love from your Valentine XX ??

Who's a clever boy in school?
OLIVER it's YOU
Who swims quickly in the pool?
OLIVER YOU DO
Who plays football?
Runs a lot?
Likes to dig in the garden plot?
Rakes the soil and finds the weeds?
Pulls them up and plants the seeds?
You're the boy who is so fine –
SO please be my VALENTINE!
Guess Who?

I'm sending you this card to say
I love You lots on Valentines Day
Be my girlfriend E-M-I-L-Y
I'll be so happy YES SIREE.
I'm waiting on the beach for you
As the tide goes in and out
I've been here for a long, long time When are you coming out?
I've loved you for so long my dear
Of that there is no doubt I sit and wait so patiently
As the tide goes in and out
Guess who sent this card to you???
VALENTINE - that's who!!!

You'll never know which song to sing
You never know what a day will bring
You never know what to cook for tea
Though you're sure to have the recipe!
And will the day be wet or sunny?
And just what happens to your money?
If you believe - I hope you do –
That all your dreams are coming true
And what will be is what will be
And I love YOU and you love me
Then everything will be just fine
Because I am your Valentine.

I like worms, I like snails too
I like muddy pies - do you?
I like to dig and make a mess
I like football, I like chess.
I do not like to be neat
I do like farts and smelly feet
Sometimes I like to go to school
But sometimes I do not
Sometimes people shout at me
I don't like that a lot
Second best of all I like
Is climbing up a tree
But best of all is loving YOU
And hoping you love me!

BIRTHDAY

Just like the girl on this card, ELLIE
Jump in a puddle and shake a WELLIE
But don't blame us if you get WETTER
Now you're five you should know BETTER!

From what we can remember
Of the dim and distant past
Being five is really great
Now it's your turn to Celebrate!

Now you are five
You go to school
You get dressed yourself
You ride your bike
Get your boots on the right feet
And you've cracked it!

Now that you are SIX
Bet you can do all sorts of tricks
Bet you can dance
And sing a song
And play at football
All day long

I only said today to Mick
"That boy is growing up real QUICK"
I know you're very good at chess
Which I can't play at all
I hear you're very good at maths
At spelling and football

And when you go to senior school
I bet you'll end up brainier
While I might even pop my clogs
Or turn out more insanier!

But if you're writing poetry
And if it all turns out to be
On every line
Much better than mine…

Then just you watch it Danny,
For your granny
Will be most put out, and shout
And even may explode, and…
Turn into a warty toad
And sit upon your head – in bed – and so…
(I just thought I'd let you know!)
(1996)

EMMA Henry, you are SIX
Can you do a lot of tricks?
Growing plants is hard to do –
WE can do it – but can YOU?
Do you know where strawberries grow?
And juicy, green peas in a row?
Do not eat too many quickly
Or you may feel very sickly.

Hello Christie
Now you are SIX
The dog on this card
Will give you LICKS
Hope you have a lovely day
With all your friends around to play
That is what birthday are for
Sent with love from the people next door.

We heard a funny story
About a boy named Rory
He had a bike which he rode all day
Though his mother sad "don't go away"
He pedalled right across the sea
He went to France and Germany
He went to Greece and also to Spain
And then he pedalled home again
He was as famous as can be
So he had jam and toast for tea.

Hello, Liam, you are SIX
The Cat-in-the-Hat will do some tricks
He'll trash the house and eat your cake
He'll keep poor Bethany awake
Your Daddy will get very cross
And then he'll show him who's the boss
He'll box his ears – I'm sure he could
And tell him that he must be good
Then that old cat will be like new
And he will be as good as you.

We once knew a boy who was SIX
He got up to a whole lot of tricks
He jumped up so hight and
We tell you no lie
He fell into a custard mix
His mum – who received a good eyeful –
Said, "Don't worry it's only a trifle."
His Dad, in the army, he really went barmy
As the custard set hard on his rifle
His brothers and sister all said
"You're a TWERP"
And the custard quite simply said
"S L U R P!"
(2002)

Hello, Catherine, you are SEVEN
That is lucky you will see
Lots of people think that SEVEN
Is a lovely age to be.
Lots of things that you are learning
Lots of things that you can do
Lots of people must be wishing
They were SEVEN just like you
We remember we were SEVEN
Such a long, long time ago
What a lot of fun we had
We don't have much fun now, you know
Our backs are weak
Our knees all creak
We can't remember who we are
We lost our memories and our marbles
We keep our medicine in a jar
We keep our tablets in a bottle
We have to take them every day
Oh how we wish that we could be
SEVEN years old TODAY

It's nice to be SEVEN
As nice as can be
To have lots of fun
Living down by the sea
It's great to be SEVEN
And it's nice for us too
For we are the ones
Living next door to YOU

You're EIGHT
That's great
Go celebrate—
Put slugs and worms on
Teacher's plate
If teacher comes and
Catches you
Don't say I told you
What to do
1998

Teddy's got the cake for Catherine
Everybody waits for tea
It's so special on her birthday
But where can gal Catherine be?
Giraffe says "I see her coming –
In her jim-jams, on her bike
Everyone sing Happy Birthday
Oh, what is that Catherine like?
Riding, riding on her bike!

Happy Birthday RORY
Now that you are NINE
You can ride your bicycle
In a nice straight line
It isn't very far to go
When you visit us
And riding on your bicycle
Saves money on the bus

Happy Birthday Ellie Faye
Now that you are nine
We just wonder who will say
They are your Valentine?
Hope you have a lovely day
For your Birthday Ellie Faye!

You'd get all "A"s
"A" because you're so much fun
So clever and so pretty
"A" because you're helpful, kind
And sporty, nice and witty.
BUT (this is where your form
Is blighted)
"Z" for zupporting West Ham United!

Now you are nine instead of eight
Bet everyone will celebrate
You must be famous there's no doubt
We can't think what it's all about!

We notice that the flags all fly
When it's the fourth day of July
And as we are akin to you
Does that mean we're important too?

Will we be rich as rich can be?
And will we win the lottery?
Will life be like a lovely dream?
Will Norwich get a football team?

Now Chase is out I'm telling you
This kind of dream might well come true
Dreams are made from this kind of stuff
That's if Mike Walker's crisp enough!

Now this is getting passed a joke
So please excuse us wrinkly folk
And have a truly, lovely day
That's all we really meant to say!

Birthday time is here again
Can't believe that you are ten!
Must be growing up real quick
Lots of love from June & Mick

Out of the world cup –
OH WELL… CHEER UP
Now you're eleven want to be ten?
Take a tip from David Beckham!
Our advice "don't get a booking –
Kick 'em when the ref's not looking"
Don't give the referee abuse –
We're senile – what's your excuse?
If Henman goes and screws things up
We'll have to wait till HENRYMAN
Brings back a CUP
But until then we'd like to say
Have a very happy birthday.

HEY YOU, Danny, thirteen you cannot be-
It's not that long ago I know since you were 1 and 2 and 3,
It's not that long, my clever chappie,
Since I observed you in a nappy
And now that I recall the s-m-e-l-l
I think it's really just as well
That you have grown up really fast
And are a teenager at last
And though it's sad to think my rhymes
Are not improving with the times,
It's nice to think you'll always be
A lovely, cutie, cuddly little kid TO ME

Micky's at a fishing match
And Rachael's here and Pippa too
And I am struggling at my desk
To write a birthday poem for you.
Now if I was your cousin
I'd congratulate you on your dozen
Or if I was your Mum
I could write you out a sum
If I was your Dad
I could tell you off when you were B-A-D
If I was your brother Sean
We could play football on the lawn
Would it be best t'play for Leicester
Or have more troubles
Forever blowing bubbles?
But then if I was Dominic James
Perhaps we'd play some other games
We'd play for Roma or Milano –
Or maybe even pay piano
But. what the heck
Here's a cheque!

Someone said that you were shifty
But I thought "that can't be true"
Maybe what they said was nifty
Yes that does sound more like you
Did they notice you were wiffty?
(That's when you took off a shoe)
Well it really is a mystery
Surely you cannot be FIFTY!

Here's wishing you a HAPPY BIRTHDAY
Hope you have a lovely day
Wish that we could send a fortune
(but you'll love us anyway)
Others may have won a million
But what good can money do?
One thing we can say for certain –
"IT WON'T BUY A FRIEND LIKE YOU."

Oh my, Ethel –
You do look cute
In your new, red
Trouser suit,
See the men all
Lick their lips
Choking on their
Chicken and chips!

Here's a fiver for you Douggie
Why not put it on a horse?
You are sure to pick a winner
One that romps around the course
Then a double and a treble
Till you've got a pile of dough
(Do not spend it in the BOOZER
That way it will quickly go)
Go instead to buy some tickets
Then you'll win the lottery
Don't forget your little darlin'
Down at WALCOTT-BY-THE-SEA
1995

Some Mothers can sing a song well,
And some can ride a bike
Some others get along well
With everyone alike

Some Mothers can cook and sew well
And one or two cannot
Congratulations Mother
We think you've got the LOT!

Ten, ten strong men sat near Big Ben
Ben went "ding, dong" fell on men strong

Ten men, now nine sat in a coal mine –
Got out too late, nine men now eight.

Eight men in car, car went too far
On a cliff in Devon, eight men now seven.

Seven men drank beer, heads not too clear,
Did not see bricks, seven men now six

Six men on train missed stop in rain,
Stepped on track live, six men now five

Five men, all wet, on horse put bet
One man bet more, five men now four.

Four men up tree got stung by bee
Some al-ler-gy, four men now three

Three men in park, stayed late, got dark
Fell in dog "do! Three men now two

Two men fell out, had fight – good bout -
Found when fight done, two men now one.

One man, oh dear, no one else there
Now then, Sean Len, can ONE man be TEN?

(Answer: Yes – YOU ARE – HAPPY BIRTHDAY)

Gal Junie

Now that it's your birthday
We hope that you're okay
The wind is howling all around
It's raining night and day

You have to put your wellies on
For walking up the road
For spolshing through the puddles
And living like a toad

When Dougie comes home after noon
You know where he has been
He's soaking wet from inside out
And sloshed from outside in

He sits down by the telly
To rest his aching limbs
It's ten to one when his horse runs
And odds on if it swims

Our hats and scarves have blown away
We're freezing in the lug-hole
The place is full of water
And we're going down the plug-hole

We're fed up with the weather
The wind and rain and such
We've booked a holiday abroad
We're going to go dutch (floods in Holland)

Don't let this ditty worry you
It's all made up by me
In actual fact it's fine down here
At Walcott-by-the-sea!

CHRISTMAS

When you're planning Christmas dinner
Roasted turkey is a winner
Filled with sage & onion stuffing –
This will cost you next to nothing
Roast potatoes, Yorkshire pud
All of which will taste so good
Carrots, parsnips, piping hot
(some will like them, some will not!)
Cranberry sauce can be quite tart
And brussel sprouts will make you
F – A – R – T

We haven't sent a work of art
A priceless piece of pottery
A large cheque or a bar or gold
We haven't won the lottery!

We haven't sent a golden crown
Encrusted with some jewels
A bracelet or a diamond ring—
We haven't won the pewels!! (?)

So hope you will enjoy a drink
We've sent some for you each
Please drink to us on Christmas Day
WE'LL BE DOWN THE BEACH!
1994

We really most sincerely trust
You won't make Santa bite the dust
But help him gently to the ground
- So he can bring our presents round!

(LONELY THIS CHRISTMAS) OUT IN MY BOAT

It'll be lonely this Christmas out in my boat
It'll be lonely this Christmas when I'm not afloat
It'll be cold, so cold, with no Rod to hold – this Christmas.

It'll be lonely this Christmas, lonely and blue
Without Bob beside me I've nothing to do
There's no Santa Claus – there's just 'er indoors – this Christmas.

CHRISTMAS AT SANDRINGHAM (1980s)

At Sandringham on Christmas Day
The Queen washed up and put away

Put all the kids on royal train
Said, "Play in here it looks like rain"

To driver, "Take them off somewhere—
Balmoral's nice this time of year"

A hare she took from greyhound track
And Princess Ann on Edward's back
With corgis and her husband Mark
Commenced to chase it round the park

And Fergy wore a bow so grand
Queen wound it up with rubber band
Till Fergy crying, "Oh my gosh"
Went orbiting around The Wash

Prince Andrew went in hot pursuit
With whirlybird and parachute
In freezing sea became a cropper
What could he do without his chopper?

The elements were somewhat spartan
For royal prince in kilt of tartan
Who somewhat gamely danced a jig
In North Sea on the Bacton rig

In front of mirror Lady Di
Was heard to give a worried sigh
So mortified she'd put on weight
(Indeed she was a large size 8)

Prince Charles cried, "It was those mince pies
But try this on my dear for size"
And being quite a royal charmer
He screwed her in a suit of armour.

Queen Mother thought she'd quickly shoot
Off down the Women's Institute
While Margaret said, "I'll get my bags
I see we've just run out of fags"

Prince Phillip had acquired a sub
And went off boozing down the pub
Where all the local men did sup
To get out of the washing up.

With smile of triumph on her face
The Queen made for the smallest place
Oh what a treat when nature called
To know one had T.V. installed

And sitting down upon her throne
Prepared to watch her speech alone
A little knock came on the door
A gentle, little knock, no more
A little voice, "excuse me ma'am
Just popped in with your OLLYGRAM"

WYMONDHAM FIRE STATION

Please don't ring the fire bell on Christmas Day
This is what the children always used to say
My daddy is a fireman and has to go away
If you ring the firebell on Christmas Day

One dark and snowy Christmas Eve
Santa Claus was stuck
Fast inside a chimney pot
But what a bit of luck
Wymondham Fire Station
Left their celebration
Set off in their fire truck
What an aggravation

Leske and MacRoberts, Gibbs and Elliott
Tried to pull poor Santa from the chimney pot
Hammond pushed and Gardiner pushed and so did fireman Skelley
Fireman Smart and all the rest were pushing Santa's belly

Everybody shouted, "Ready, steady go"
Santa came unstuck and then they all fell in the snow
We hope it will not happen but one thing we all know
If there's an emergency the fire bell must go.
1979

BEFORE PROCEEDNG

Before proceeding along this driveway, please note the following by-laws
All cars must be driven through an antiseptic dip (Dettol preferred)
Toll fee 50p per car (not to exceed 4 occupants)
Pedestrians must wash feet before entering (a bowl will be found under the hedge) OR slippers maybe he hired £1 per hour
Cats are strictly, absolutely and positively FORBIDDEN under all circumstances
Bicycles must be locked and left outside the entrance and must be of presentable appearance, roadworthy and no rust.
Parking fee payable see pay & display meter
Milk bottles should be carefully polished and newspapers ironed with the sport page uppermost (in the event of N.C. suffering a defeat this rule may be waived).
Current passport or NCFC membership card should be carried and Norwich City colours worn at all times.
The management would prefer Liverpool or Ipswich supporters refrain from entering within one mile radius of the driveway. Thank you.
I hope you enjoy your visit & wish you a Merry Christmas.

MERRY CHRISTMAS FOLKS

Here's wishing you a happy journey
Through the year that is ahead
Without too many hills to climb
But with an easy road instead
We hope you have a happy Christmas
With all the things you wish come true
Good health and happiness forever
As this is what we wish for you.

ART

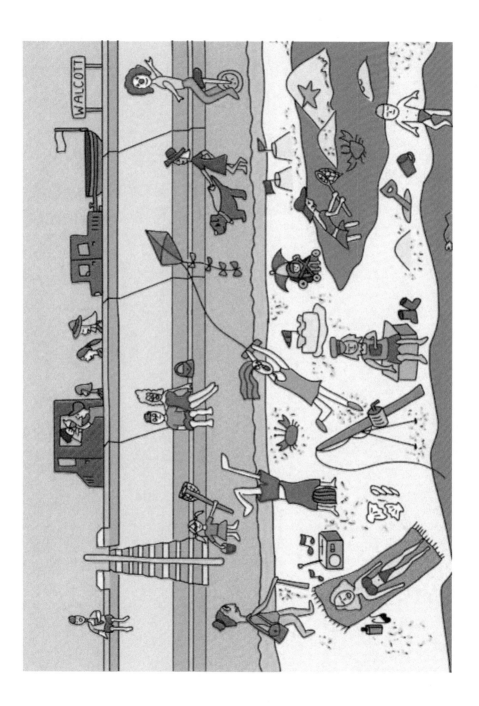

Gal Junie

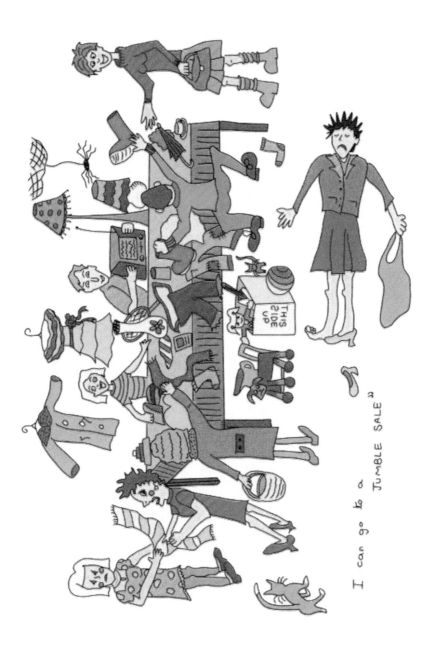

STORIES

PIPPA'S SEAT

Jack and Thomas wanted
to watch a video but
Pippa had the best seat...

Mummy said,
"Please take this old
jumper to Auntie Ra-Ra.
It will keep her hedgehogs
warm"

Auntie Ra-Ra was so
pleased she said,
"Please take these magazines

to dentist Roy for his
Waiting room."

Dentist Roy said,
"These are just what I
Needed. Please take this
old white coat to painter Jim."

Painter Jim's old overalls were full of holes. He
was so pleased and gave

Jack and Thomas some paint for Pippa's kennel.

Thomas and Jack painted
Pippa's name on her kennel.
She was very pleased and settled down for a sleep.

Thomas and Jack ran indoors
to watch their video but ...
Pippa had the best seat!

GIRLS AT THE FOOTY

"Take us to the footie Uncle Jamie"
begged Molly and Catherine, 'we
want to watch the Canaries playing"

"Sorry" said Uncle Jamie "but you do
not dress properly for the football"

Molly and Catherine went to their
school jumble sale and were soon kitted out.

"I still can't take you" said Uncle Jamie
"because you do not know what to sing"

Teacher, Uncle Jeff, taught them to sing "On the Ball City". He said they were both very good.

Uncle Jeff took them to the match at Carrow Road. The Canaries won 3-0 and everyone cheered and sang.

Jamie couldn't go to the match, he had to baby sit with little Emma. "Take me to the footie Daddy," she cried.

A POEM OF THANKS TO GAL JUNIE

Dear friends just a letter of thanks
For putting on your naughty pranks
We would like you both to know
How much we all enjoyed your show
I went to Marks and Spencers
To buy bloomers like you had on show
But I am sad to tell you
They just didn't want to know.
Your music too was very good
I have to tell you that
With my little block of wood
I found my notes were flat
Talents like yours are all the rage
You should both be on the stage
Our friend George and I enjoyed every bit
We had the giggles and were ready to split
I even went to the jumble sale
For drawers with a hole in the middle
I wanted some like Grandma had so she could do a pi__le!
I am sure our George and all
Hope it won't be long
Before you make another call
And sing another song.
You friends at the day hospital bid you adieu
And not without a big thank you!

ABOUT THE AUTHOR

Gal Junie was a pre-WWII baby born and raised in Norwich, Norfolk. Bombing raids hit her home, so her family evacuated to the country, in Wymondham. Besides a few years in Melbourne, Australia, Gal Junie has always lived in Norfolk.

Her compilation of odes, stories and songs span the era of bringing up her own family and taking her 'show', with her sister, to the 'old folks' clubs and care homes, providing some laughs, entertainment and many sing-a-longs to some golden oldies.

Now an 'oldie' herself, she has compiled this book of her odes, original songs and unique birthday and Christmas messages to her family over the years.

You'll soon have your favourite 'O'de June'. Perhaps the humorous "Ronnie's Fishing Hat", the fun song "Patricia's kisses" written for her daughter, or the more poignant "Poor Old Joe", now featured in her daughter's novel, "Redway Acres - Helena".

Printed in Great Britain
by Amazon

58267581R00089